BULLSH*T OR FERTILIZER

BULLSH*T OR FERTILIZER

A Portable Pep Talk

Pierre Bennu

**Andrews McMeel
Publishing**

Kansas City

Bullsh*t or Fertilizer

03 04 05 06 07 MLT 10 9 8 7 6 5 4 3 2 1

ISBN: 0-7407-3316-8

Library of Congress Catalog Control Number: 2002111552

THIS IS

AN INNER CHILDREN'S BOOK

done especially for you by the friendly folks at exittheapple productions.

Text and drawings by pierre bennu.

Edited and laid out lovely by jamyla bennu.

Special thanks to mirlande jean-gilles for inspiring page 57!

THIS BOOK
IS DEDICATED TO

my wife,

for existing on this earth
at the same time as me;

my mom,

for showing me how
to live with or without;

my superhero friends,
for constantly inspiring me;

my student loan;

and you,

for caring enough about yourself
to save the world.

CONTENTS

AUTHOR'S NOTE

I'm writing this book because I'm tired of having this conversation.

It's a compilation of ideas, advice, and collected wisdom gathered from dozens of e-mails, phone calls, and discussions I've had over the last two years.

It is a self-help book. To me, that means, "You gotta help ya damn self." I can point you to the library but I can't do your research for you. I present you with my truth because it's been helpful to me and to a lot of my friends, but I can make no guarantees.

You can see it as bullshit or fertilizer.

But Pete, Why Is It so Little?

I never understood why books don't just get to the damn point. I remember being in college and reading fifteen pages of text to highlight two lines. I'd be like, "Why didn't they just say that?"

This book is not for stupid people.

In other words, I'm not gonna spell out everything.

Highlight this whole book. Because it won't be long, and it'll be right to the point. As a matter of fact, here's the first point, free:

You can do anything!

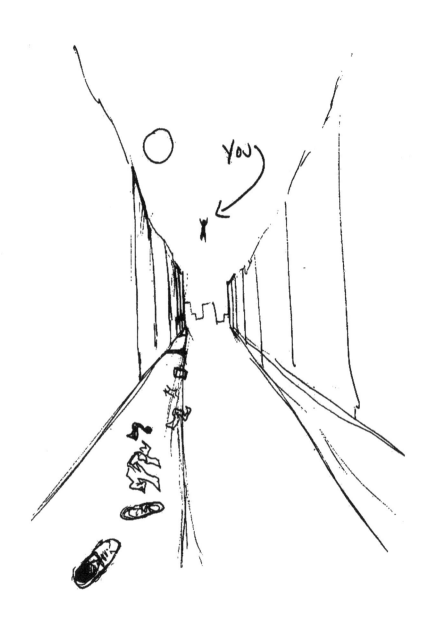

THE LEAP:
Learning to Fly

We are surrounded by dreams. Everything you see—from the street to the cars on it, from the ice cream to the cone you eat it from, from the shoes on your feet to the way you wear your hair—someone invented that; it was once somebody's dream.

"It" always begins with dreams.

Remember that!

"It" is going to be coming up a lot in this book.

"It" = Whatever you do. Your craft. Your work.

Living in New York City can put a lot of things into perspective. Whether you want to be a singer, writer, actor, or whatever, there are thousands of people who want what you want, too. And they've come from all over the world to get it. So the question is never really how much talent you have, it's more about how bad do you want it? What are you willing to risk?

You are what you DO.

If you have no product relating to your art (no chapbook, no Web site, no portfolio, no demo tape, no reel, no painting, etc.) then you do not exist in this reality as that thing. For instance, if you work as a secretary and wish you had time to sing, then you are a secretary. **You are not a singer.** A lot of us do what we don't like for money and call it "work" and feel uncomfortable getting money to do what we love. It does not have to be this way.

You can live off your craft.

People do it all the time.

A lot of artists I know with children speak about how the birth of their child made them serious about their work.

Why wait?

Take your work as seriously as you would take a new life.

People put faith in the stupidest things.

Here's an example. What if I said this:

> Hey, reader, let's go into a hundred-year-old tunnel
> thirty feet under a centuries-old city to ride an elec-
> tric train beneath a river and thousands of tons of
> concrete and steel buildings?

Your likely answer would be **hell, no!** But millions of people ride the New York City subways every day without a thought, and we actually think that we're getting a deal! It doesn't occur to us to doubt; we're just thinking about our destination.

We choose our fears.

If you're scared about It, it's because you choose to be.

Dear Reader:

You are a divine being sent to Earth to save the world. First you must realize that you are the bomb. Your mission is to help the rest of the world figure it out. But before you can do that, you have to claim it for yourself.

Open doors.

It's futile to look at the present state of the arts and say "There's less soul/integrity/etc. in art these days." I used to get upset when my favorite artists would change their look, style, or sound to fit with what was hot when it clearly wasn't them. Then it came to me: When someone you admire starts to suck, you should see it as an open door. They suck so you can shine. There's a void and they're giving you room to enter.

Divorce yourself from outcome.

If you get caught up thinking about whether you're better than someone else or if the world is or isn't "ready" for what you have to offer, your work will never get done. So what if a few people laugh at your cape and boots? You're SuperWo/Man.

There are a lot of people who have the audacity to be untalented or ignorant or unimaginative out loud and in public. We need to be the superheroes we know we are in public, too. The world is falling apart and we choose to play Clark Kent: sitting at a desk with a cape on underneath our work clothes. You are here to create balance. All you have to be is you— out loud.

My suggestion: Buy a Superman T-shirt. Rock it.

If you don't like your job,

quit.

That means:

Trust your work enough to hire yourself.

A moment of courage can mean a lifetime of joy.

It's hard work . . . but it's work you're doing for you.

But BEFORE YOU QUIT . . .

You must *be* at least as organized as the place you work. In fact, you will have to *be* **more** disciplined to get your own *ball* rolling. Have a net before you leap. Make a plan. (See page 67.)

SPEAK IT 2 YOU
Language as a Tool

Words are a tool with which you *speak* your reality. If you say you are ugly, or lazy, or pitiful . . . then that's what you are. If you say you are magical and blessed and successful . . .

Here are some exercises and definitions to help you reshape the way you speak.

15

Stop talking about people, especially people you hate.

Who do you like? Who do you admire? Speak their name constantly, instead. Speak of the good that people do. Did you know Dikembe Mutombo gave $3 million to start a hospital in the Congo? That's some shit! Talk about that.

Be your own fan.

Wake up in the morning, look at yourself in the mirror, and say something affirming like, "I'm the bomb."

Because you are.

My suggestion: Try it naked!

Don't talk in "I'm gonna's" or "I want to's."

Example: "I'm gonna write a book." "I want to sing someday."

My advice is to not say anything. Don't call it; just do it. Let the project speak for you. A ticket to your show or an autographed copy of your new CD or book speaks volumes more than small talk. If you must talk about it, speak about completed work. Like, "I just finished my third song/chapter/draft/etc."

Stop saying "I don't know" when making decisions.

And if you really don't know something, learn it.

The next time you're asked "How are you?" try answering in the extreme affirmative.

"I'm amazing." " Wonderful! "
"Life is great!"

It's remarkable the reactions you get from people. It's also a good opportunity for you to count your blessings, because if they ask for clarification, you're put in a position to tell them why this day is wonderful.

I highly suggest this exercise.

Transform your language.

"Making   it"   =   _____

_____

_____

_____

_____

_____

_____.

Define what "making it" is for you. It doesn't have to mean
making $34 million a year; it might mean living comfortably
without debt or doing what you love for a living or living with
integrity.

"Sanity Tax" = Money set aside to use for fun events, toys, clothing, or entertainment. **Fun is mandatory!** It prevents you from going crazy.

"Broke" = "My money is presently tied up in other investments." My suggestion is never to use the word. You ain't broke; you're whole.

"Deadline" = "Birthdate." I recognize the corn factor here, but it's taken a lot of stress out of my work process to think of due dates as dates of birth.

"Silence" = The period after you've put in all your work, when you're waiting for results. Trust that the work you've done will yield fruit. Trust the silence.

"Active Procrastination" = Anything that you do that is not "It."

Example: You want to make an album, so you start selling fried fish. Your plan is to open a fried fish restaurant and have an open mike night. And when the restaurant is popular enough you will sell the CD from the kitchen.

But before you do that, you have to go to chef school and business school, and the next thing you know, you're mixed up in a world that has nothing to do with what you really want. You do it under the pretext of "working toward your goal," but you're not. You're actually procrastinating.

EDITING
Transforming Your World

You call the people around you lazy and destructive? You say they talk too much and never **do?**

Well, that might be true. But my challenge is to always check yourself first. The people around you are a reflection of something within yourself—they reflect what you allow, aspire to, or settle for.

The following steps are in no particular order. You can fill in the numbers in the order that you do them.

STEP ____

Get your phone book right now.

Get a black permanent marker.

With the exception of family, mark out anyone's name who is not helpful and/or supportive of your goals. All your friends should have something to do with "It," even if it's just encouragement. If they don't inspire you as much as you inspire them, they are vampires feeding off of your spirit.

It sounds harsh, but just see how refreshed you feel when they're not calling you anymore.

My suggestion: Cut off anyone who tells you, "You can't." (Yes, her too.)

STEP ___

Figure out your costume and your headquarters.

A fireman wears a fireman suit and works out of a firehouse. A doctor wears a white lab coat and works out of a hospital. What do you wear? What does your space reflect about you?

I suggest giving your clothes to charity or your friends. Or you can go through your closet with a pair of scissors and cut everything in half that does not reflect who you have chosen to become.

Find a scent that makes you feel good. Get your incense/oils/perfume/candles on. Scent is often overlooked, but it makes a difference.

STEP ___

Treat your space with reverence.

Treat your clothes with the respect that you would like to be approached with. Iron your shirt—even if it's a T-shirt. When you take it off, don't just drop it on the floor; fold it. Hang it up.

Do a thorough scrubbing of your living/working space every season, **not** just in the spring! Make a weekly ritual of cleaning your space.

Take the garbage out before you go to sleep.

STEP ____

Ask yourself every day what have you done to get closer to your goal.

Note: This might make a good journal. You can probably use it as a memoir when you "make it."

STEP ____

Thank your body, verbally or otherwise. If you are sick, talk to your sickness. Let your body know your plans and that you need its cooperation. You are not your shell, but you do have to live there.

My suggestion: Buy a book on wholistic medicine and/or natural cooking and/or vitamins, please!

STEP ____

Do **not** make yourself miserable out of obligation or to please others. That includes your family, your friends, people you owe money to, your boss, etc. It's not worth it.

STEP ___

Turn off the damn TV! Next time you watch TV, glance at the clock and time how long it takes for you to hear or see something negative. Network television pays its bills by selling advertising*; so it's all as sensational as possible. Take it all with a grain of salt— even the news, much of which is run by the same corporations that do most of the ugly in the world. But that's another book.

---

*Special note on advertising: The whole point of advertising is to make you want things you don't need. They do this by making you feel imperfect or incomplete. Be wary of messages like "Obey your thirst" or "Gotta catch 'em all." I actually saw a sports drink ad that proclaimed it "has the stuff that water doesn't have." **What?** Do yourself a favor and determine your needs for yourself.

May I reiterate: Turn off the damn TV.

STEP ____

Be still.

STEP ___

Find a reason to laugh hard every single day.

DO! DO!

Practical Stuff

DO! DO! Health

Waking

Remember Eddie Murphy in **Coming to America**? He woke up to violins playing and bathers with rose petals at the foot of his bed. What a wonderful way to wake up!

The way you start your day is usually how your day will go, so make sure that it's good. If you lack bathers and a personal orchestra, a CD that you like and a few minutes spent stretching can do wonders.

My suggestion: Make a tape of your favorite music and call it your theme music.

Have it with you as much as possible.

Eating

I'm not heavy on telling folks how to feed themselves, but I do believe you are what you eat. Always look at ingredients. If it's fast food or something with no ingredients listed, you should probably steer clear of eating it too often. Eat what you like, but love your body and feed it well. Fuel it so it runs as efficiently as possible.

My measure of fitness is generous: If you can't dance, you might want to consider having that burger without the cheese.

Rest

Know your limits. Take a break. Chill.

Watch some cartoons, play a video game, sit in a still, dark room; do whatever it is that relaxes you. Turn off the phone and rent some movies, catch up on those shows you taped, or just take yourself out on a date.

Though it might sound cool to say, "I've been up three days," or "I was up all night working on this project," if you burn yourself out and can't complete it, your late nights won't matter.

DO! DO! The Work

Don't think of your friends as customers.

They're your friends . . . and they're probably artists, too. They might buy your CD, but then you're gonna have to buy theirs when it comes out, so it's really just a recycling system.

If you want to develop an audience/readership you've got to move outside of your circle of friends, no matter how supportive they are. Go to a new town; enter a new scene. Your friends will support you. That's what friends are for.

If you want to do something that hasn't been done yet, make a way. If you can't find a way, you don't want it bad enough.

Do it yourself.

You can't get hired as an actor *because* no one appreciates your "look"? Didn't get into that dance troupe *because* you got too much bootie?

Start your own acting collective! Start your own dance troupe! Make connections with other people doing work that complements yours.

Talk to your local independent filmmaker who always needs talent to work with. This goes for filmmakers and directors, too. Go to auditions . . . there are always more people dissed than picked. You can just go and hand out your business cards, if nothing else.

Don't do it to death.

Deal with legalities, copyrights, etc., but don't obsess. Getting the legal stuff together can easily become active procrastination.

I've heard people say, "Yeah, once I get the money to incorporate my business, then I'll start to get my act together."

That's ridiculous. Your focus should be on doing your work and getting it out there. It's better that you are seen and have product than to eternally be in the lab waiting for the right time to "come out."

Fun is mandatory.

Make sure what you do is fun for you, or you won't "make it."

Work to keep it fun.

Ideas don't wait for you.

Have you ever had this happen? You had an idea and slept on it. Then two months later you *see* or hear about somebody having done "your" idea.

That's because ideas are all energy and flow freely. Until you put your name on something and manifest it in the world, it belongs to no one.

Please don't let that discourage you, though. If you had an idea and it's been done already and you are still feeling it, still **do** it. Just because she made a song about menstrual cramps doesn't mean you can't. She's not you, and you might bring a different flavor to that topic.

Rule of thumb for business relationships: If people are "too busy" to return your calls, if they show up late to more than one meeting, if they talk more than they can show (they're a "producer" but can't tell you anything they've produced), then cut them off.

That's all. No discussion necessary. If they clean up their act, they know how to reach you, but **do not hesitate** to move on.

The "let go" theory.

So you messed up? So what! You're probably going to mess up a million times before you become an Old Pro.

Just make sure you understand why you messed up. Take note of it. Write it down, if possible. Did your computer crash with all your old work on it? Well, sheeeeeit. It's time to write some new work! And in the meantime, you've learned a valuable lesson about saving and backup.

There are no mistakes.

Remember that your product represents you. Packaging is important. Don't be afraid to hire someone to help you.

Once you have your product, carry it on you at all times. If opportunity comes along you want to have something to hand it.

You don't want that thing to *be* in your car; you want it on your person. Not at home, either . . . **on your person!** A CD of your music, a *book* of your paintings or photographs, an excerpt of your novel should be in *easy* reach. At the very least, always *be* ready with a business card.

Mi Suȷȷeshȷun: "They" no dat U R N R-tist. Yew don't have 2 spell stuph "creatively" to get dat poynt akross.

Interview yourself.

Ask yourself questions about your work, and answer them. This will solidify your conception of what you're doing and why. When asked, you should be able to articulate yourself with grace and accuracy.

Don't be afraid to do this out loud and in public. If people look at you and wonder what the hell you're doing, strike up a conversation with them. Hey, they're a potential audience member!

The college thing.

Many people feel pressure to go to college. I've found that in most art-related fields, experience is often as good a teacher as books. It's not always necessary to have a college diploma validate your field of study.

If you're already in college or have interests that take you there, I advise you to buddy up with someone who's not in your major and learn something you didn't pay for.

A note on the buddy system: Ask someone to do this book with you. Call or meet and keep each other on point. Encourage and support each other.

DO! DO! Money stuff

Until you get a manager, you must act as your own. As manager, your job is to make sure your artist is happy, fed, living comfortably, and producing work.

Be on yourself like a manager would. Advocate for yourself like a manager would. Ask yourself the tough questions: Would you hire this artist? Would you recommend this artist for a prospective gig? Is this artist versed enough in his or her craft to be represented by you?

Become one with your inner manager.

Grants are your friends.

Go to the library, the foundation center, the Internet.

There are millions of art, community, and foundation dollars each year that go unclaimed. These dollars are there for you.

Do the research.

Know your worth.

Here's an idea: When asked "How much?" quote higher than your last job. Let them talk you down if they must but know that if you state it with confidence, they probably won't.

Once a month you should do what I call "doing the math." Sit down with your partner or with your receipts and check out how much you have spent in each of the following categories.

- Sanity tax

- Food

- Transportation

- Investment in your craft

- Rent/bills

- Clothes

- Stupid shit (know yourself)

This exercise will help you discover what your spending patterns are and you'll be able to budget more efficiently.

Buy it if you need it.

I say spend *because* if you live in lack, you will attract and generate lack. If you live in abundance, you will attract abundance to you.

Trust your gut on what going overboard is.* Put a budget together for clothes and grooming, and after you decide what it is, don't slack.

*This is not an excuse to go crazy. You know what I mean: You need new shoes to go with your new look, because that's part of the package of You. But you don't need twelve pairs of new shoes; not today.

Here are a couple of money-saving tips to consider when making a purchasing decision if your funds are presently tied up in other investments.

- If it's a book: Unless you **need** the book to help you in your craft on a daily basis, **use the library!** It's free. They have videos there, too.

  - If you only need these "corporate disguise" shoes for one event, can't you buy a bootleg copy at Payless?

  - If you're feeling guilty, you probably don't need it.

  - Between thrift stores and garage sales, you can find almost anything. Check them out.

  - With the list of friends you have left after your editing exercise, ask yourself if you can borrow it.

Ask yourself these questions.

How much money have I made from my craft this year?

In the past six months?

Who/where does it come from?

How can I make more?

Barter.

Supporting other artists is as important as making art. Feed folks, buy them this book, give constructive feedback, exchange work, lend them money, bring them juice when you go over to their house. We have to make this world as comfortable for each other as possible.

How about this: Send five people who have inspired you a check for $5 each. (Yes, more $$ would be fine if you got it.) The important thing is that you include a handwritten note explaining what they did that helped you and how it helped you. Trust me, it will make a difference for them to know.

NEW GROWTH
Stuff to Think About

Two homeless men were asking for money on the corner. One asked for a dollar and a passerby gave him a dollar. The other homeless man said, "Hey, since you're givin' out money, can I have a hundred?" The person dug in his pocket and gave the second man a hundred!

The moral of the story is **you get what you ask for.**

The key is, when you ask the universe for what you want, be sure to be as detailed as possible and clear in your intentions.

Writing it down is a great way to clarify what you want. You can even post it up somewhere in your space and work toward it.

We live in a

violent, ugly

beautiful, peaceful

chaotic world,

that needs

you

RIGHT

NOW.

Disbelieve in lack; it is an illusion.

There is enough.

Don't be in competition with anyone but **you.**

Scarcity is "rich-folk" hype to keep "poor folk" living on top of each other.

Don't believe it.

There's enough space, food, and money on this planet for everyone and it's not naive to think so.

The past is the last breath you took. You can start over right now.

Helping people is beautiful and rewarding.

Do it often. We all need a little help.

However, volunteering, "giving back," and extending your time and your energy to help others can turn into active procrastination, too. Make sure to volunteer to help yourself, too. One of the best ways to help people is by being successful.

You must take risks.

You are not promised tomorrow.

Do it today.

Pick someone to love.

Tell somebody that you love them at least once a week, if not every day. A friend, a lover, a family member . . . let them know. Not because you expect it back but because love is meant to be given.

Get into the habit of giving.

Don't assume that people know how to love and choose to be evil instead.

Some of us haven't seen the alternative.

Be that alternative.

THE MAP
Because You Have to Have a Plan

You got plans, and God's got plans. No one is leading the exact life that they planned out.

All that considered, you should still have a plan. A syllabus, if you will. It will help guide your movements and make it possible for you to evaluate your progress.

Begin with the end. What do you want to have done, and by when? That's your goal. Start with that goal and work your way back to where you are now. Map out your steps in as much detail as possible.

Let's use a songwriter as an example. The goal is to complete a CD in a year.

Before a CD can be cut, you need a studio. (Call friends with home studios; save money to rent studio time.)

Before you go into the studio, you need to rehearse. (Set aside six hours per week for rehearsal.)

Before you rehearse, you will need a band. (Find musicians. Cajole or compensate them for playing with you.)

Before you have a band, you need to have songs written. (Get up off your ass and write them!)

So what are you waiting for? Get started!

Tips

Brainstorm about different ways to complete each step. Remain flexible.

If you have a circle of very smart and supportive friends, it might help to invite them over for a brainstorming session. Then afterward, there will be the bonus that they know your goals and schedule and will be able to help keep you on point with check-up calls, etc.

The map should include due dates. You need to know whether you're ahead of or behind schedule. It should include a completion date for exposure of your work to the public in as PUBLIC a space as possible. The local open mike is fine for starters, but the point here is to let the world know, not just your friends.

To generate dates, assign your steps to a timeline based on the total time and then give yourself further detail.

January–February: Manage your time. Write songs. Look for musicians.

March–June: Finalize your band and begin rehearsals. Set up gigs for summer.

June: Band is ready for studio (halfway point).

June–September: Begin gigs; the money from which will go toward studio rental.

September–November: You're recording.

November–December: Find distribution/representation. Build a Web site.

I'm no singer, so this is a rough sketch just to show the mapmaking process. You've studied your craft. You know what you need to do and what is reasonable to expect of yourself. Know your process. Don't force it.

More Tips

After you make this map, put it up somewhere you will see it every day. A good spot is near a calendar.

Don't plan too far into the future—I say three years, tops. That gives you enough room to grow, but not enough to get distracted in the possibilities. The purpose of this plan is to guide your actions now. Even a newborn is old enough for daycare in about three years. A lot of change and growth can happen in that time!

I just want to give some special shout-outs to a couple of specific genres.

Deejays: Roam your neighborhood and pass out your mix tape to local stores that play music.

Writers: Start a writers' circle. Meet regularly or share writing through e-mail. Write every day.

Actors: Put your day jobs on your resume. What, you weren't acting in Kmart, the temp job, or the soup kitchen? A little creative renaming goes a long way.

Comics: Remember they are here to see you. Don't be nervous.

Dancers: Start your own dance class at a local YMCA.

Painters: Throw your own show. If you can't find a gallery, you know somebody with a backyard or a restaurant in the neighborhood or a bigger apartment than yours.

Designers: Make designs for businesses that don't exist. It builds your portfolio and it's fun.

Everybody!

Don't take professional advice from amateurs.

Don't be afraid to ask—let everybody know what you're up to and what you need. You'll never know who can help you unless you ask.

AFFIRMATIONS
You CAN Handle the Truth

Understand the logic behind affirmations.

In a world of media saturation, we are bombarded with imagery and subliminal messages. Your home should be a place where you are bombarded with messages of your own creation.

When something outside of yourself affirms what you are, it helps solidify your vision of yourself as that thing. If you hear somebody say you're a great dancer enough times, you start to believe you are a great dancer. Give yourself permission to be great— don't wait for it from others.

Affirmations in your house are like you creating an outside influence on yourself. You should have at least one in every room.

Here are some ideas.

- Yes.

- The universe has my back.

- I can do anything.

- Nothing is too good to be true.

- Stay fearless.

- I am worth it.

- Failure is not an option.

- There is enough.

- I am beautiful.

- Let go!

- Be curious.

- I am loved.

- I am limitless.

- Pleasure is everywhere.

- Don't worry.

- Trust in God.

- Stay at peace.

- I am whole.

- There are no mistakes.

- I am everything I need.

- Creativity flows through me.

- Speak love.

Repetition is a powerful tool.

Remember when you got in trouble in school and had to write one hundred lines? The same principle can help your creativity, too. Whenever I doubted myself, I'd write, "I am a filmmaker" over and over until it filled up the whole page. Doing this helps get you into the habit of affirming what you are.

On the next pages, write over and over, "I am a brilliant and prolific _____," or something equally as affirming. Affirm "It."

After you're done, put this book down.

_____

_____

_____

_____

_____

_____

_____

_____

_____

_____

_____

_____

_____

_____

_____

_____

_____

_____

_____

_____

_____

_____

_____

_____

_____

_____

_____

_____

_____

_____

_____

_____

_____

_____

Okay, that's enough. Now you're actively procrastinating. Go do your work!

YOU CAN DO ANYTHING!